LEEDS

THE ARCHITECTURAL HERITAGE

A FIRST SELECTION
PHOTOGRAPHED BY IAN BEESLEY
COMMENTARY BY GEORGE SHEERAN

RYBURN PUBLISHING

First published in 1993
Ryburn Publishing Limited
Krumlin Halifax

Produced and printed by Ryburn Book Production, Halifax, England

INTRODUCTION

When people think of Leeds, many probably conjour up the image of a northern city built on the profits of the woollen industry, and it is true that Leeds owes its early prosperity to wool textiles. By the late middle ages and during the 16th century a great trade in woollens had grown up and a merchant community resided in Leeds busy in the export of woollens via the port of Hull to the continent. By the 18th century, the Leeds merchants had a reputation second to none, and had raised the town to a position of pre-eminence in the county for mercantile trade and commerce. It was their houses, mostly built in fashionable classical styles with proud elevations to the street, that dominated the town; it was largely the merchants who paid for the building of the new churches they attended; and it was through their generous donations that the town's cloth halls came to be built.

But if many in Leeds made their livings by the wool trade, we should also remember that to the east of the town several important landed estates could be found. Foremost was Temple Newsam, home of the Earls of Lennox, and from the 17th century the Ingrams, the Viscounts Irwin. The Saviles, ennobled as the Earls of Mexborough, had their seat at Methley Hall. There were also the Hastings and Whelers of Ledston Hall, the Blands of Kippax, the Lowthers of Swillington and the Lane-Foxes at Bramham, not to mention a larger number of less substantial, though, important gentry. Thus Leeds benefited from both worlds: from the profits of trade and commerce, and from the patronage bestowed by noble and gentle families. By the end of the 18th century, Leeds was a town consisting of two cloth halls, several handsome churches and many shops, workshops and inns, particularly along Briggate. To the immediate north and west of the centre were the houses and grounds of merchants and professional families, while small tradesmen and the lower orders tended to live centrally or to the south and east. By this time Leeds probably occupied the position confirmed by the 1801 census – fifth most populous town in England. It was, moreover, a developing town, yielding only to Manchester, Liverpool, Birmingham and Bristol in the size of its population, and to none in the ambition of its merchants.

Changes were already taking place. First, by the end of the 18th century a greater number of people were employed in trades or industries other than the woollen industry. Secondly, Leeds was already entering the first stage of its industrial revolution as factories began to appear. Among the first, and certainly the largest, was Benjamin Gott's at Bean Ing, a steam powered woollen mill, and this was followed by many others. The production of woollens, however, was not the only textile industry. Linens had become established during the early part of the 18th century, and largely through the technical expertise and enterprise of John Marshall, the spinning of flax by power became of immense importance during the first half of the 19th century. Indeed, during the middle years of the century the textile industry began to diversify into several areas, especially dyeing and finishing and the production of clothing.

With the growth of machine production in textiles throughout the county, and with the coming of the railways in the 1830s and 1840s, the engineering trades of Leeds began to flourish. There were also well-established glass and china manufacturing industries. Most surprisingly, although the merchanting of cloth remained important, the town was to lose its position as the mercantile centre of the West Riding to Bradford. But if this door began to close another opened to allow the spread of commerce and financial services, with large numbers of insurance offices, brokers and banks locating their offices in Leeds, especially in the district around Park Row. By the last quarter of the 19th century, the character of Leeds had changed. It was a centre of commerce rather than mercantile trade. It was as well known for clothing production as for the manufacture of textiles. Its foundries and engineering works produced thousands of textile machines, steam engines and railway locomotives; they made agricultural implements, constructed steam hammers and cast bridges. It was a thriving commercial and industrial city with most of its industry located south of the River Aire in a strip running from Armley in the west to spill over into Holbeck and Hunslet to the south.

It was smoke from this industry that, even from dates early in the 19th century, led residents on the more fashionable western side of Leeds to complain about the nuisance it caused as the prevailing wind carried it in their direction. This was eventually to lead to a relocation of the middle class suburb much farther to the west in Woodhouse and Headingley. Contrary to this westward flow, working class houses were built mostly to the north and east of the town centre and across the river, to the south, in and among the factories and heavy industry of Holbeck and Hunslet. At the same time, the centre itself became crowded as the yards and courts of older buildings were filled with cheap cottages.

Leeds in the 19th century had all the classic problems of the rapidly expanding northern industrial town: overcrowding, epidemic diseases, poor water supply, inadequate sanitation and a high death rate, particularly among children. While historians have been correct in observing an awakening of the social conscience and a movement towards reform, there was little immediate impact on Leeds, and the majority of the working class continued to suffer the ills of poor housing and industrial pollution. So much so that a shocked writer in *The Builder* in 1860 condemned Leeds as "filthy and ill-contrived", as a place where housing had not kept pace with population growth and where the working class endured worse conditions than their masters' horses. The article ended with the challenge, "Millionaires of Leeds! you are your brothers' keepers." But unlike fellow entrepreneurs in towns such as Bradford and Halifax, the magnates of Leeds did little of a substantial and lasting nature to ease housing and other social ills.

Thus 20th century Leeds contained many problems, the worst undoubtedly being the amount of slum property. The city centre, on the other hand, was a place developed in the best traditions of Victorian architecture and planning, with many grand buildings and displays of civic pride. Indeed, the core of Leeds remains Victorian. But the attitude of the 20th century towards this architectural heritage has not always been kind. In this respect it has been little different from the 19th century treatment of Georgian Leeds. Like their Victorian counterparts, our planners and developers have razed areas of the centre with scant regard for what was already there. But every generation holds in contempt the architecture of the immediately preceding generations. Who knows, given time, all those soaring concrete and glass buildings that many people now dislike may come to assume a dignity and a place in the affections of our grandchildren.

In the 20th century we find ourselves in a unique position. We have two or three hundred years of architecture in our city centres, a heritage that we are capable of conserving, and which we should not allow to be destroyed. But we will surely be condemned if we hand on to posterity nothing of architectural value from our own century. It is a question of what is appropriate: of conserving the best, the most typical and the useful, and building the new. In common with many other towns and cities, Leeds could be accused of ruthlessly pursuing the latter course in the 60s and 70s. While redevelopment of the city centre continues (as it has, of course, in every period), a more careful approach has been adopted in recent years in which the value of much 19th century work has been taken into account, and street landscapes that are already satisfactory have been preserved.

This work presents a selection of some of the best and some of the most typical of the buildings of Leeds. If it concentrates on the 19th century, then this is because the overriding impression created by Leeds is that of a 19th century city. This is not to say that we have completely ignored the modern. Twentieth century buildings are included in the selection – buildings which, despite some criticisms, we believe are among the best to have been erected in Leeds in recent years.

George Sheeran

Kirkstall Abbey

The earliest and most important medieval building in Leeds is Kirkstall Abbey. Tradition has it that Henry de Lacy, a powerful landowner of Norman descent, had promised to found an abbey in thanks for his return to sound health. He instructed the abbot of Fountains Abbey to look for a suitable site at Barnoldswick, but the abbot lighted on the Aire Valley close to Leeds as a likelier spot. Whatever the truth of this, Kirkstall Abbey was founded in 1152 by the Cistercian Order, and seems to have been largely complete by 1175. It comprises a complex of buildings surrounded by grounds amounting to about fifty acres. Its importance lies in its being little altered over the centuries from its original plan. Its planning was similar to Fountains Abbey with a nave, aisles and transepts, but unlike Fountains it has a tower raised above the crossing, a tower that was heightened in the 16th century. The detailing is rugged with little ornamentation as befitted the Cistercian discipline, perhaps. The east window, like the heightened tower, dates from the 16th century.

Kirkstall Abbey Gatehouse

In 1539 the Abbey was dissolved, and the gatehouse was converted to a dwelling for the last abbot, John Ripley, who died in 1568. Formerly visitors would have passed through this building to gain access to the Abbey and its grounds, but the gateway itself was blocked to form living accommodation.

Over the years, and particularly in the 19th century, the gatehouse has been altered and extended, but the 12th century vaulting of the gateway can still be seen internally. The gatehouse is now the Abbey House Museum.

St Peter's, Kirkgate (R D Chantrell 1839–41)
The ecclesiastical history of Leeds itself must inevitably start with St Peter's, the parish church. There had been a church in Leeds since before the Conquest, and by the 14th century it had grown into a large building containing five altars. By the 16th century it consisted of a nave, chancel, aisles and transept with a tower above the crossing. In the next two centuries it became filled with box pews and, to accommodate more people, galleries were fixed along the nave. This was the state in which Walter Farquhar Hook found St Peter's when he became Vicar of Leeds in 1837. Hook and his architect Chantrell were responsible for the church we see today. Chantrell's rebuilding of St Peter's produced a spacious, open feel that contrasted with the clutter of the old church, yet retained links with tradition, being built in a gothic style. Unusually, the tower is placed in the centre of the north front, rather than at one end or above the crossing. The rebuilding was completed in 1841, when the church provided a fine stop to the view along Kirkgate.

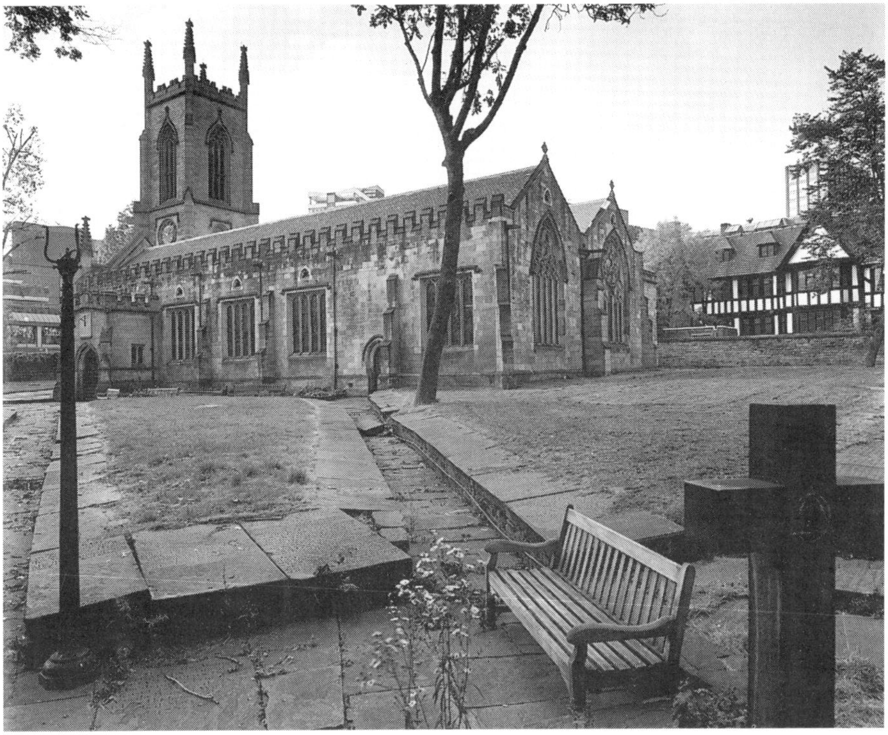

St John the Evangelist, Mark Lane (above, below and overleaf)

St John the Evangelist, Mark Lane

St John's presents us with that architectural rarity, a 17th century church. While it is not true to say that church building ceased after the dissolution of the monasteries, it undoubtedly slowed, and as far as Leeds is concerned, no ecclesiastical building had appeared since alterations to St Peter's in the early 16th century. As one of the largest towns in the country, Leeds could support more than one Anglican church. In 1631 work began on St John's, and it was consecrated in 1634. The design remained true to West Yorkshire traditions of building, using square-headed mullioned windows, buttresses and battlements that could have been found on churches built a hundred years earlier. But at the same time, the original porch had a typically Jacobean strap-work crest, and much of the internal woodwork and plasterwork conformed to local traditions. During the 19th century the church underwent extensive restoration, and although much of the exterior fabric was preserved, the interior was stripped of a good deal of its woodwork. Fortunately, much of the woodwork was rescued during the last century and returned to St John's.

Holy Trinity, Boar Lane (William Etty 1722–7)
Leeds was a growing town and was judged to need a further church by the early years of the 18th century. A scheme for a new church was mooted by some leading merchants of the town, but it came to nothing through lack of subscriptions. It was revived when Lady Elizabeth Hastings of Ledston Hall contributed £1000, and by 1722 a foundation stone had been laid. Holy Trinity was a rather exclusive church with a congregation composed of many of the merchants who had subscribed to its building or purchased pews there. The architect was William Etty of York who designed the church in a mannerist style – notice how arches or keystones break through the floors of the pediments above them in deliberate contravention of classical patterns: this is not a lack of knowledge, but breaking rules to effect. Originally the tower had a spire, but this was replaced by R D Chantrell after storm damage in 1839.

St Saviour's, Ellerby Road (J M Derick 1842–5)
Dr Hook has already been mentioned in connection with the rebuilding of St Peter's. Hook's influence on early Victorian Leeds – he was vicar between 1837 and 1859 – cannot be overstated. During his ministry he built twenty-one churches and twenty-seven schools, extending Anglican influence into the surrounding suburbs. His acquaintance with Canon Pusey, a leading member of the Oxford Movement which tried to restore the High Church traditions of the 17th century, led to the building of St Saviour's. Pusey himself is thought to have made a substantial donation towards its construction. The Decorated style and cruciform plan – originally a tower with spire was planned for the crossing – made it an important Gothic Revival church owing to its scholarly adaptation of medieval design. However, the spire was never built, and its proposed name, the Church of the Holy Cross, was changed in deference to the Bishop of Ripon who thought it too Catholic-sounding. Today, therefore, the church lacks the spire that would have given a dramatic vertical emphasis to the composition. One of the most attractive aspects of St Saviour's is the vicarage (to the right) a modest, but delightful, Gothic Revival design, much enhanced by the retention of its chimneys.

St Bartholomew's, Armley (Walker & Athron 1872)

St Bartholomew's is set prominently and dramatically on the skyline to the west of the city. It is built in a style transitional between Norman and Early English with a high nave and a tower set on the crossing. The tower, with crossing and apse clustered tightly around it, is its most arresting feature and it supports a short octagonal spire and four bold pinnacles at each corner. St Bartholomew's is one of the few churches within the immediate vicinity of Leeds which still stands in a large open area that was its churchyard and burial ground, and it retains one or two graves of well-known Leeds families – the daughter of Joshua Tetley, for example. This makes the decision to extend the nearby telephone exchange all the more lamentable, since British Telecom's impenetrable slab of brick now obliterates the view along Church Road.

Mill Hill Chapel, Park Row (Bowman & Crowther 1848)

Nonconformism in Leeds has a lengthy history – Celia Fiennes had commented in 1698 "this town is full of Discenters". The first nonconformist chapel seems to have been the Mill Hill Chapel built by the Unitarians in 1672. This was a neat early classical building probably rebuilt in a more ambitious classical style in the 18th century. But by the mid-19th century, the demands of an increasing population called for greater accommodation and the chapel was completely rebuilt in 1848. This new chapel made an historic break with tradition for it was in a gothic style, a well-handled Decorated, whereas most nonconformist chapels and meeting houses were classical, shunning the forms associated with the established church. To this end, a severe classical frontage with plain sides often suited the bill. But Mill Hill changed all this and in Leeds it marks the date at which gothic styles became acceptable to nonconformist congregations.

Mill Hill Chapel now stands as if in an historical oasis, surrounded by some of the more arid designs of the 1960s and 1970s. But from some angles the chapel enlivens this dry functionalism, as above, where both buildings gain something from the juxtaposition.

Salem United Reformed Church, Salem Street (1791 onwards)
The Salem Chapel was built in Hunslet Lane in 1791 but has undergone several rebuildings. The original chapel is now masked by later additions, although the side of it still contains its original windows along Salem Place, and it seems to have been a plain, classical design of building. In the 1860s a Sunday school was added in an Italianate style, right. Further extensions took place after the turn of the century when, in 1907, a remarkable curved front was added

to the original chapel front. This is a hard piece of neo-classicalism, so studiously anachronistic that one could be forgiven for thinking that it dated from the 1820s. The Salem Congregational Institute was built in 1908. This was one church that was not converted to native gothic, a rather more austere classical style being preferred despite a flirtation with the Italianate in the mid-century.

VOL
I
HYMN
BOOK
HOLY
BIBLE
MATTHEW ELSWOR

New Wortley Cemetery

While Leeds had no shortage of churches in the 19th century, the shortage of graveyards was an acute problem, and a number of private burial companies were formed. New Wortley Cemetery came into being after the middle of the 19th century and in 1903 it was remodelled and furnished with new gates and mortuary chapels. It is situated on the side of a bank overlooking Holbeck, Hunslet and New Wortley and its occupants went to their final resting places above the great industrial morass of the Leeds engineering and textile industries. There are few large and impressive tombs here, many of the graves being those of tradesmen. Most have headstones with a round or pointed arched top and are carved with flowers, birds and texts such as "Thy Will Be Done". Occasionally, one comes across a rather more unusual headstone such as the one dedicated to Matthew Elsworth who was a carrier, or the one to Christopher Joseph Shaw who died in 1879 and was evidently connected with the locomotive industry or railways.

Temple Mills, Marshall Street (Joseph Bonomi 1839–43)

The great increase in the population during the 19th century resulted in pressure on space which was particularly severe in the industrial towns. The population of places like Leeds grew through both natural increase and the attractions its industries held for migrant workers. During the first fifty years of the 19th century, for instance, Leeds became the most important flax spinning centre in Europe. John Marshall was the son of a prosperous Leeds draper who had begun flax spinning in 1788 at Scotland Mill, Meanwood. But it was on a new site at Water Lane, Holbeck, that he began experimenting with the machinery and new production methods that were to make his fortune. These older mills were routine designs with little to recommend them architecturally. However, in 1838–9 he was persuaded to extend his business, and engaged Joseph Bonomi to design an office block and a mill, a commission which Bonomi carried out in an Egyptian style. The mill itself was a new concept in design – it was of a single storey, and insulated from the the effects of the weather to provide an equable

temperature and humidity suitable for flax. It thus contained a ventilation system. The design of the office block draws heavily on the great Ptolemaic temples at places such as Edfu, Esna or Kalabsha in Egypt. Above the entrance is the horbehuted or winged sun emblem of the goddess Rat, thought to protect buildings from collapse. Unfortunately this did not stop the original obelisk chimney from cracking in the 19th century. On the other hand, Temple Mills today stands intact, a startling sight amid the industrial dereliction of south Leeds.

Tower Works, Globe Road (attrib. Thomas Shaw 1864)
As Bradford rapidly overhauled Leeds as the centre of the textile industry, the economy of Leeds diversified into dyeing, finishing, tailoring and engineering. Railway locomotive engineering was especially important and so was textile machine making. Much of this heavy industry was located to the south of the city in Hunslet and Holbeck. Although a great many buildings have been torn down in recent years, some of the best have survived, and the chimneys of Tower Works stand out as a landmark. The works was established by Thomas Richards Harding whose early years were spent in France where he began to manufacture wool combs. In 1853 he returned to England and around 1864 seems to have built Tower Works where he manufactured hackles, combs, cards and various pins for linkages. Much of the works, possibly designed by the Leeds architect Thomas Shaw, has been demolished but the screen wall and entrance survive.

The chimneys are the chief ornament of the works. The finest, with an octagonal top, was perhaps taken from Sir Robert Rawlinson's "Designs for Factory, Furnace and other Tall Chimneys", a volume which supplied the inspiration for several factory chimneys in West Yorkshire, including the chimney of New Mill at Saltaire. The design is decidedly Italian and seems based on the Torre del Commune at Verona. A further chimney was added in 1899 when the firm was under the control of Harding's son, Thomas Walter, and his partner. Designed by William Bakewell, this chimney was based on Giotto's campanile for Florence Cathedral. There is also a third chimney, a simple square-section shaft, which lacks both decoration and the tapering profile of most chimneys. It probably dates from between 1892 and 1900. Could the Hardings or their architect have been thinking of the topless, slighted towers that are such a feature of San Gimignano?

New Crown Point Printing Works, Hunslet Road (Thomas Ambler 1894)
Printing is one of the areas of 19th century industrial growth which is often overlooked. Mass-circulation newspapers and magazines, calendars, advertisements, packaging and labelling, not to mention cheap novels, all produced work for the nation's printers. By the second half of the century new techniques of photographic reproduction were being commercially developed. This led to cheap, high-quality illustrations, a branch of the industry that had previously relied on more expensive engraving or lithographic techniques. Of particular importance in this

respect was colour printing. Alf Cooke had become a printer early in life, producing illustrated almanacs from a works in Hunslet Road. His colour printing was of such quality that in 1885 he was appointed chromo-lithographer to the Queen. He was singularly accident prone: two of his factories burned down, but the third, built in 1894 near Crown Point, survives. Here, Ambler designed a long building with a deep but brightly lit printing hall. The main accent of the building is on the corner entrance with its clock, Cooke's monogram and originally the Royal Arms above the door. The body of the building sweeps along Hunslet Road.

The Electric Press, Cookridge Street

Many Leeds firms were engaged in the cabinet making and upholstery trades, some supplying cheap furniture for the lower middle class, others making high quality pieces and art furniture for the wealthy group of professionals and manufacturers. The best known firm of Leeds cabinet makers was Marsh, Jones and Crib, whose premises on Boar Lane have now been demolished. Another outstanding firm was Charles Roodhouse and Sons, a firm which came to prominence in the 1860s when it moved to the premises seen above. This is a simple but effective design for a cabinet works and warehouse. Built of brick with stone dressings and bands, it seems to have been based on Venetian palace designs of the 16th century which have been reinterpreted in a highly simplified manner. Roodhouse and Sons moved to Albion Street around 1897, but had ceased trading by the early years of this century. The works were taken over by Chorley and Pickersgill, printers and binders.

Leeds and Liverpool Canal Office

Much of the early trade and industry of Leeds was supplied by navigable river or canal. From early days the River Aire around Leeds had been navigable, and in 1699 the Aire and Calder Navigation was established by Act of Parliament in order to facilitate the movement of goods around Leeds and Wakefield. The big change came, however, when a scheme for a canal connecting Leeds and Liverpool was proposed. In 1770 an Act allowing the construction of the canal was passed, and by 1775 a length of canal was open between Leeds and Gargrave. The whole canal was completed in 1816. During the present century the Leeds end of the canal had become run-down, but it is now being rehabilitated and retains some of its older buildings, among them the canal company's offices. They have a small, but dignified front, showing modest neo-classical influences such as the tri-partite windows. They date from perhaps the late 1770s or 1780s.

Canal Warehouse (Robert Owen 1776)
Only a little of the former character of the canal wharves remains, for a number of the warehouses in this part of Leeds have been demolished. Today it is difficult to imagine a crowded waterway with its boatmen and labourers busy with cargoes. One early warehouse

has survived, however, on the south side of the canal. It dates from about 1776. It is stone built, four storeys high and has a regional appearance in its detailing – the mullioned windows, for example. Each storey steps back very slightly as it rises, probably in an attempt to strengthen the structure by providing a thick and stable base.

Crown Point Bridge (Above; George Leather & Son 1842)
Leeds Bridge (Overleaf; T. Dyne Steel 1871–3)
Victoria Bridge (Opposite; George Leather 1837–9)
Access to Leeds from Holbeck and Hunslet in the south is hindered by the River Aire. Until the 19th century only one bridge crossed the river, taking the highway from the south into Briggate, one of the main thoroughfares of the town. Old prints of the area around Leeds Bridge show it clustered with warehouses and wharves and the river thick with boats. This area also became the most heavily industrialised quarter of Leeds with factories eventually

spreading down to Hunslet in the east and along to Kirkstall in the west. By the 1830s, the inadequacies of one river crossing could no longer be tolerated and two new road bridges were constructed. The first of these was Victoria Bridge in 1837, named after the new queen, followed by Crown Point Bridge in 1842. Later, in 1871, Leeds Bridge was rebuilt. Crown Point Bridge is perhaps the most handsome. It retains its open gothic ironwork sides, a feature inspired, no doubt, by its proximity to St Peter's, the parish church. The surrounding area has mostly been cleared of 19th century industry along with its working class terraced houses but it is debatable whether the result is an improvement. We seem to have exchanged a labyrinth of houses and run-down factories for a complex of roaring roads and wastelands, made even more anonymous by the lack of street signs in places. It is a bewildering sight, lacking recognisable human activity other than the relentless flow of traffic. In recent years attempts have been made to improve parts of it around the canal and river, for example by the building of the new Asda premises and the conversion of some warehouses to dwellings. Hopefully, this process will continue.

Wine & Co.

The Corn Exchange (Cuthbert Brodrick 1860–62)
The major commercial building in Leeds, and indeed one of the finest pieces of Victorian architecture in the country, is the Corn Exchange. Although the commercial and industrial reputation of Leeds rested on the clothing and engineering industries, it should be remembered that the agricultural produce of the county was bargained over, bought and sold in the town. An earlier corn exchange stood just off the Headrow near its junction with Briggate, but this had become too small by the mid-19th century. In 1860 the corn factors of Leeds and the Markets Committee held a competition for the design of a new exchange to be built on a site next to the old White Cloth Hall, and Brodrick's entry won. It is an elliptical domed building, majestic and monumental, constructed of diamond-pointed rusticated masonry throughout. If monumental, the building avoids being ponderous by the lively animation provided by the rhythm of repeated round-headed windows.

Corn Exchange interior

The Corn Exchange now houses a variety of specialist shops in what were originally the factors' offices; access to those on the first floor is provided by an elliptical gallery. The ground floor is huge and unimpeded by columns or other structural members, since the roof is a dome, part-glazed to provide top-lighting. The roof itself is constructed on a radiating

sequence of arches intersected by the side beams or purlins. Brodrick's genius in buildings like this lies not so much in his originality – the Corn Exchange is quite clearly derived from the Pantheon and Roman amphitheatres via influences from France. It is more his masterly sense of proportion and the crisp, vigorous lines of his structures that mark him out as an architect of the first rank.

Bank of England, South Parade (Philip Hardwick 1862–4)
Leeds became a centre for banking and financial services in the 19th century, building on a foundation laid in the previous century. The pre-1800 Leeds banks had usually been run by families connected with the mercantile trade of the town, and in large part existed to serve the needs of the clothing industry. This role was now extended and Park Row and streets in its vicinity became the commercial and financial heart of the town. Here one could find banks, insurance companies, the Leeds Stock Exchange and also the Bank of England. The latter was designed in a heavy classical style with channelled rustication to the ground floor masonry and a Roman Doric portico. The stern appearance this gives to the building seems appropriate given its position as a branch of the nation's premier bank.

Leeds and Yorkshire Assurance Co [Britannia Building Society], Albion Street
(W B Gingell 1852)

Rather less sombre is the building in Albion Street that was formerly the offices of the Leeds and Yorkshire Assurance Company. The architect, W B Gingell of Bristol, had won the competition for the design of these offices, producing what was for Leeds an early and confident palazzo style. It was perhaps Sir Charles Barry who pioneered the style in the late 1830s, drawing on the classical palaces of renaissance Italy as a design source. While his palazzo designs are rather austere and based on buildings that lacked the classical orders, Gingell's design is in keeping with the more ornate palazzi of the Veneto. There is more than a hint of the palazzo that Andrea Palladio created for Issepo da Porto at Vicenza around 1550, especially in the way a rusticated ground floor with arched openings is surmounted by a columniated storey with an attic storey above. Gingell has then enriched this basic form.

Scottish Union and National Insurance Co, Park Row (Henry Perkin 1909)
Further evidence of the strength of the financial quarter of Leeds is provided by such buildings as the Scottish and National Insurance Company's offices. It was built in 1909 in a hard classical style faced in white tile. This hardness is relieved by the ironwork balconies to the first and second floor windows, and sculptural enrichment of a particularly high order. Along the second floor level, flanking the entrance, we find half-naked females presiding over Fire and Life, while along the Park Row elevation, Commerce and Wisdom reassure the passer-by. Despite the obvious quality of the finish, I find this an undisciplined building. There is an irritating lack of balance between the Park Row and South Parade elevations, and there is a clash between the almost Art Nouveau enrichment and the austerely classical form.

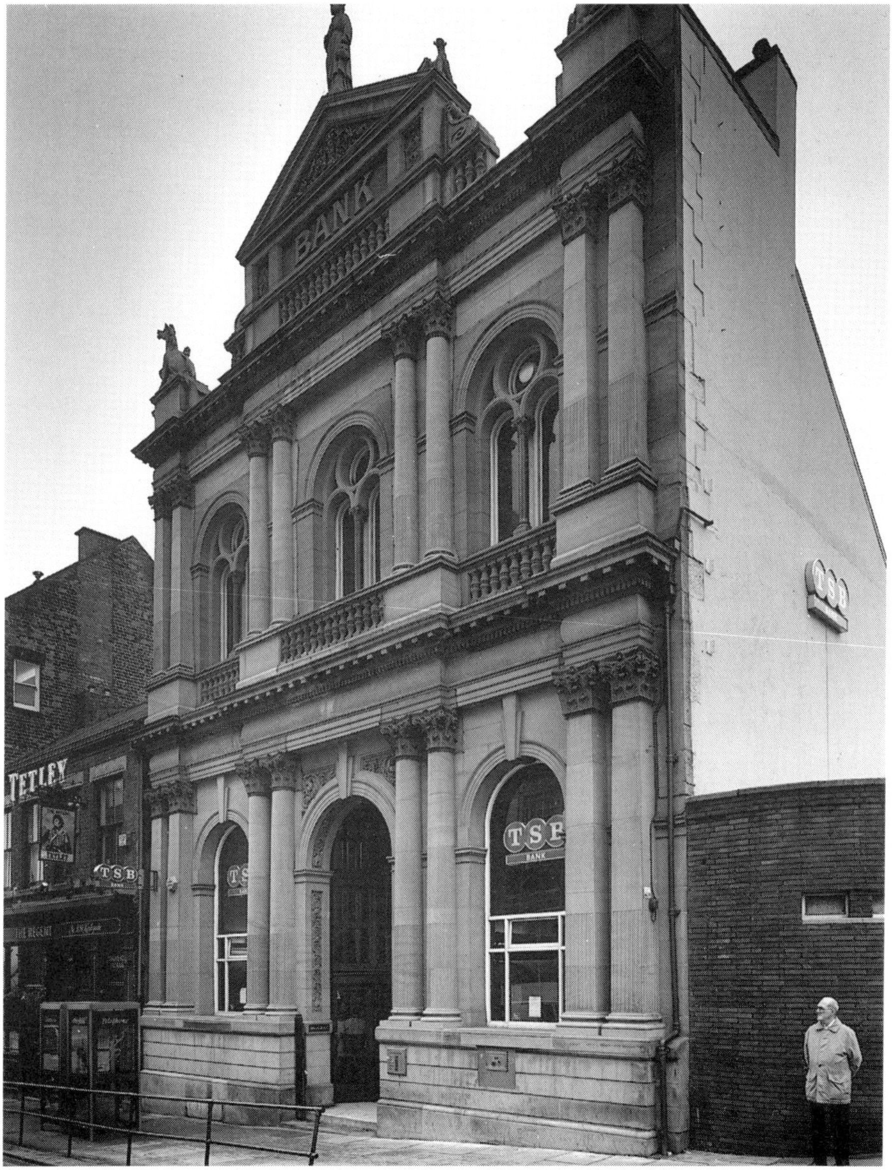

The London and Midland Bank, Kirkgate (William Bakewell 1892)
Not all the banks were located near Park Row, and some companies opened branches late in the century in other parts of town, such as the London and Midland Bank. This building, near to the market, is interesting for a couple of reasons. First, it shows the persistence of the Italianate style. Bakewell's bank is a conservative design that might have originated in the 1860s: only the elongated keystones of the ground floor windows and perhaps the little pediment above the eaves suggest a later date. Secondly, it shows the degree of erudition of some Victorian architects. The design draws on the the architecture of Venice, but not the well-publicised gothic Venice of Ruskin's *Stones of Venice*. Rather, it recalls the architecture of the renaissance city and architects like Mauro Coducci. Victorian architects gained such knowledge only by painstaking study and first-hand experience of buildings in Italy.

30 Park Place (Thomas Ambler c.1863)
Before 1800 it was common for merchants to build warehouses adjoining their homes. Here cloth might be finished and packed for export. But the 19th century brought changes as mass-production separated home and work, and as some manufacturers began to merchant their own wares. Such changes led to the building of specialised warehouses for home or export markets, containing their own office suites and located near to railway goods yards. Foreign merchants also set up businesses. 30 Park Place was built for N P Nathan, an important German export house with branches throughout England. The character of most Leeds warehouses is gothic, and Ambler's design is no exception, having a Venetian Gothic air in its pointed arches and shafts, together with Italianate tracery heads to the windows. But he freely mixes other elements into the design. At any rate, this was Ambler's original intention, but insensitive alterations over the years have resulted in the removal of some of this detail. Nevertheless, it is one of the finest of the Leeds warehouses.

1 & 2 York Place (attrib. Stephen Smith c.1870)

It would be misleading, however, to think that all the Leeds textile warehouses were built in gothic styles, for a small number are classical, such as this pair at York Place whose first occupiers were woollen merchants and manufacturers. The basic constructional form – a series of tall arches supported by piers with windows between – suggests that the architect was thinking of ancient Roman buildings such as the Aula Palatina at Trier. The facade is ornamented with decoration drawn from further Roman sources: the stone sills, for instance, that connect the piers between floors and below windows are carved with paterae and recessed diaper patterns. The stonework of these sills also provides a contrast with the plain brick walls as well as a horizontal accent across the verticals.

Leeds Bridge House
Westgate Point

This pair of buildings is worth considering for the ways in which 19th century architects and 20th century architects have responded to the same sort of problem. Both were built on difficult sites intersected by busy roads. Leeds Bridge House was originally a temperance hotel built around 1880, but later converted to several commercial uses. Westgate Point, built in the 1980s, is the offices of one of the city's oldest legal firms. A little over a hundred years separates them, yet it is interesting to see that the problems of the sites have been solved in similar ways: notice, for instance, how both buildings allow their thinnest ends to make the greatest impact. Furthermore, both are built in Italian-derived styles. By the second half of the

19th century Italianate styles had become so thoroughly absorbed by British architects that they were second nature, and designs could be turned out with great skill and facility. Leeds Bridge House is a good example, showing confidence and verve in the design of a five-storey building on a difficult wedge-shaped site which is also extremely slim. By the beginning of the 20th century the Italianate style had been largely abandoned, to be rediscovered in the late 1970s and 80s. Westgate Point is an early attempt to come to terms with the style in a post-modern context. It should, perhaps, be forgiven some of its faults: the massing leads to an awkward junction on the north side, the detailing is flat, and the architects have failed to solve the problem of draining the deep, overhanging eaves other than by converting a series of down-pipes into etiolated brackets.

The Queen Victoria, Great George Street

The busy commercial life of Leeds led to a demand for places of refreshment and lodgings. From perhaps the middle ages, and certainly the 16th century, Briggate had become the location of numerous inns. This is given testimony by several visitors to the town, who sometimes commented on the Yorkshire hospitality on offer there: "any body that will goe and call for one tanckard of ale and a pinte of wine and pay for these only, shall be set to a table to eate with 2 or 3 dishes of good meate ..." wrote Celia Fiennes in 1698. As the town increased in size in the 19th century, large numbers of inns and public houses were built in the same traditions. The Queen Victoria is a beautifully preserved example of the 1860s, built in a chunky gothic style with shafts to the doorway and first floor windows. The inscription "Family and Commercial" advertises the respectable nature of the business.

Metropole Hotel, King Street (Chorley & Connon 1897–9)
By the later years of the 19th century, Leeds had grown to such importance that there was a need to provide luxury accommodation for numbers of visiting businessmen, dignitaries and others for whom public houses or inns could not provide the standard of service required. Hotels of this sort had been developing from early in the 19th century, especially at the spa towns and seaside resorts. But hotels in provincial towns and cities developed somewhat later. Chorley and Connon's Metropole Hotel dates from 1897. Built in a gigantic and freely interpreted Queen Anne style, it gives the impression of strength and weight, an impression created by the use of giant consoles to support bay windows to the upper floors. The walls are a mass of deep red terracotta enriched with swags and cherubs in places and striated with banding. The effect is a frenzy of texture. The stone cupola has been reused from the fourth and last cloth hall which had once occupied the site.

Thornton's Arcade (George Smith 1877–8)
As Leeds developed in the 19th century, the narrow yards and passageways behind the main streets became built-up with squalid dwellings and workshops. Towards the end of the century, a number of these yards were cleared and converted to shopping arcades with glazed roofs. The first seems to have been Thornton's Arcade, named after Charles Thornton, owner of the White Swan Inn which stood on the site. The gothic frontages to the arcade are simple, even primitive in appearance. Within, the pointed arches of the new shop fronts are repeated in the roof trusses. One of the novelties of the arcade is a clock with mechanical figures in medieval costume striking the hours.

County Arcade (Frank Matcham 1898–1900)
If Thornton's Arcade is the earliest of the Leeds 19th century arcades, County Arcade, the last, is the best. It stands in Vicar Lane on a site that the corporation was eager to clear, but which was acquired and developed by a private company, the Leeds Estates Company. They had commissioned Frank Matcham to design a new shopping complex which he carried out in

a free Jacobean style using a mixture of brick and Burmantofts faience tiles enriching this with marble and onyx. Matcham was an architect of skill and acclaim, known best for his theatre and music hall designs (e.g. The London Coliseum, London Palladium). Perhaps his experience in the design of these buildings and the associated problems of mass-circulation led him to create an arcade which, although broad in its span, provides an unencumbered floor area. In fact,

there are two arcades which cross in the centre, above which Matcham placed a dome, thus increasing the feeling of spaciousness and light. In 1875 *The Building News* had written that "railway termini and hotels are to the 19th century what monasteries and cathedrals were to the thirteenth century". It is an observation that might well have been made of the markets and arcades of Leeds.

Leeds Town Hall (Cuthbert Brodrick 1852–58)
Leeds was among the first of the West Yorkshire townships to build a town hall in the 19th century. The old Moot Hall had become inadequate for the town's needs, but it was not until the middle of the century that a new building was considered necessary. The position of Leeds as one of the five largest towns in England demanded a building more in line with Hansom and Welch's Birmingham Town Hall (1830s) or H L Elmes's St George's Hall at Liverpool (1839–40). It is surprising then, that the thirty-year-old Cuthbert Brodrick, a newcomer to the town,

should win the competition for the design of the building in 1852. Brodrick's town hall is in the grand French manner of classical architecture, containing all those elements that he so obviously admired. The front is composed of two end pavilions connected by a long Corinthian colonnade. To show this elevation off to better effect, it was raised above a rusticated basement approached by a broad flight of steps. Originally the building lacked its tower, but Brodrick's design was changed several times during the course of building, concluding with the great baroque colonnaded tower in which the town bell was finally hung in 1860.

The town hall interior boasts a similar magnificence, as seen in this illustration of the main concert hall with its cylindrical vaulting and panelling, not to mention the great organ. The embellishment – which preserves the original designs of John Crace – is of a scale and richness that accords with this huge vaulted space. While Brodrick was probably well aware of

St George's Hall in Liverpool, one wonders whether he was also familiar with some of the other great neo-classical interiors that seem to be echoed in his design – the library at Sledmere, for instance, a place not too far from his native town of Hull.

Municipal Buildings, Calverley Street (George Corson 1876)

To accommodate the growing amount of municipal business, it became necessary to construct further buildings. In 1876 a competition was held for these new Public Offices, as they were first called. They were to house various departments together with School Board Offices and a reference library. George Corson won the competition with a design in an Italo-French palace style which relies heavily on the use of the Corinthian order and arcaded windows to the extent that wall surface has been virtually eliminated. It was a sound design which did not attempt to compete with Brodrick's Town Hall, but harmonized with its French influences and the order used. However, as *The Building News* reported later in 1877, the design was modified: it was heightened to three rather than two storeys and its length was shortened. This had the effect of destroying Corson's well-proportioned original – the tinkering hand was as much at work in the 19th century as it is today.

The real eye-opener is the interior which feels like a Venetian palace and Romanesque church mixed with essence of fantasy. Mosaic floors, marble shafted columns, sculpture and tiles combine in a rich effect along the double staircases of the building. Arcades and iron grille-work provide views across from one staircase to another, creating remarkable spatial effects. It is the best of the Corson interiors, and yet it leaves one feeling bilious: as if one had consumed the whole menu instead of carefully selecting. Calmer and more successful is the reference library, illustrated overleaf.

Here, beneath a timber arch-braced roof, book presses are located in an arcade. This runs around the central hall of the library which has a gallery above. At the far end, the head of Shakespeare looks down from the pediment of a press – not so much in reverence, but stuffed and mounted as part of the Victorian cultural bag.

The School Board Offices, Calverley Street (George Corson 1880)
The shortening of the new public offices cut out the School Board Offices and they were added as a separate building in 1880. The Education Act of 1870 had enabled the formation of school boards and this naturally meant that in a municipality the size of Leeds considerable office space was needed. In the School Board Offices, Corson reworked his original design which was this time built with the top storey he had intended. The main entrance makes the greatest impact with a deeply recessed, highly arched portal framed by Corinthian columns between antae or piers.

City Art Gallery, The Headrow (W H Thorpe 1887 onwards)
The last of the 19th century municipal buildings was an art gallery, built in 1887 adjoining the reference library and facing the Headrow. It was an insipid design by W H Thorpe, with thin classical detailing. Blomfield obviously recognised the problem in the 1930s when he provided plans for the widening and remodelling of the Headrow: he proposed a new facade for the gallery, but his plan was not carried out. It was not until 1980 that a new gallery fronting the

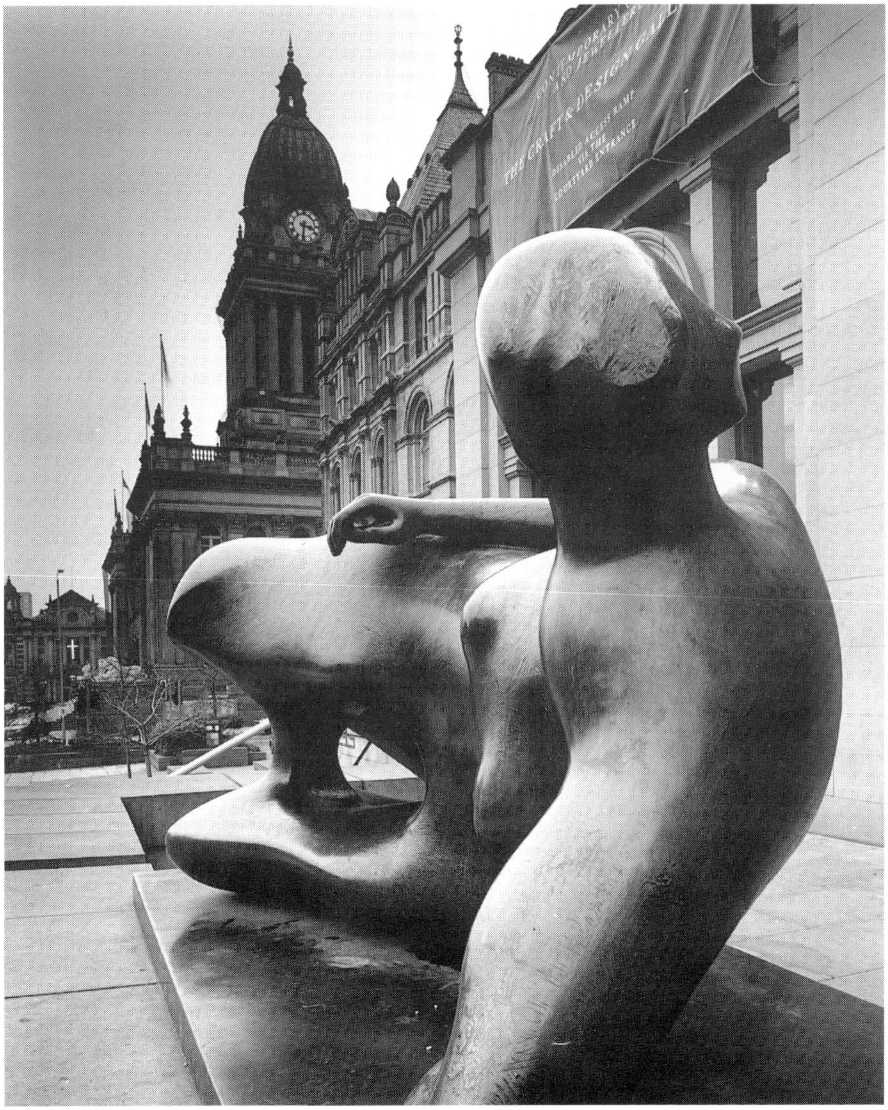

old was built. This was a sculpture gallery, named in honour of Henry Moore. The building provoked controversy: some found it an offensive piece of botching that destroyed the front of the old building, and it has to be admitted that the new gallery does not key into the earlier buildings with complete success. However, the old front was no great loss. The new, in chaste ashlar, works well in context: it takes the eye from the uncarved block, through the rippling textures of Corson's buildings to the grandeur of Brodrick's Town Hall.

Civic Hall, Calverley Street (Vincent Harris 1933)
Further municipal buildings were added in the 20th century, on a site to the rear of the Town Hall. Civic Hall housed more council offices and a suite of reception rooms. The building abandons Yorkshire stone, Leeds brick and terracotta for that favourite 1930s material, Portland stone. The more important buildings of Leeds constructed between the wars had all used it – the Queen's Hotel or the University, for example. Civic Hall is a startling composition framed by twin towers surmounted by obelisks – the owls on top are from the civic arms. There are also stripped classical elements, such as the simple pavilions decorated with discs halfway up the towers, which contrast with the vigorously-sculpted putti lower down and the general baroque feel. It is touches like this, together with the odd-ball clocks on brackets and the slightly wide spacing of the towers, that create a feeling of unease in the design, yet have contributed to a unique landmark in the city's architecture.

Armley Board School, Armley Road (Adams & Kelly 1878)

The Education Act of 1870 enabled local authorities to make provision for children's education. After this date we see the formation of school boards and a good deal of school building. The Leeds Board provided some large schools, the early ones designed mostly by the partnership of Adams and Kelly, architects to the Board. This school at Armley is a fair example of their style, a symmetrical Italianate design in brick with stone dressings and a central campanile. The aim has been to create an imposing building – but are the proportions right? The wings are perhaps too thin in relation to the body of the school, and the same might be said of the ground and first floor pilasters. The addition of a portico supported on spindly columns has not helped matters.

The Mechanics' Institute, Cookridge Street (Cuthbert Brodrick 1860–65)
Before state and locally funded education was available, numbers of private institutions, from dame and factory schools to grammar and public schools, catered for the need. To supply what we might think of as further education there were the mechanics' institutes. Strictly speaking their origins were located in the ideal of self-improvement, and it seems likely that the first ones emerged in West Yorkshire during the 1820s. They existed to serve the educational and moral needs of working men, and as such tended to be funded not only by the better-off sections of the working class, but also by local philanthropists eager to exert a

measure of social control through education. The Leeds Mechanics' Institute can trace its origins back to 1825. By the 1850s its popularity was such that new premises were needed, and in 1860 Brodrick supplied a design for a new institute on a site near the Town Hall. There was a lecture room, gallery, studios and classrooms, all contained within a French-influenced building. It is given a commanding accent in its great central portal, to which the other elements of the design are subordinated. Carved in the pediment are tools of trade and symbols of art. As with his design for the Town Hall, the body of the building is displayed on a rusticated plinth or basement which has been battered (inclined) for greater effect.

Quarry House, Quarry Hill (Building Design Partnership to be completed 1993)
Quarry House is one of the most powerful architectural statements to be made in Leeds. It stands more or less on the site of the former Quarry Hill Flats and is to be the headquarters of the National Health Service Management Executive and the Benefits Agency. Two things give this building prominence. Firstly, it is sited on rising ground at the far end of Eastgate and presents a lofty visual stop to the vista along this street. Secondly, the design of the Headrow and Eastgate, which were remodelled to the designs of Sir Reginald Blomfield in the 1930s, are reflected in the design of Quarry House, but on a grander scale. Indeed, this is a colossal reinterpretation of neo-classicism in which the main architectural interest arises from the

structural elements themselves and the scale of construction. Its symmetrical front has a heavily emphasised centre with a semi-cylindrical entrance balanced at either end by tall wings and apses. The lower storeys are clad in polished granite while the upper storeys are of brick with stone dressings, and contain a series of grand windows. One criticism that might be made is that the segmental pediments on the west front appear to sit too lightly on the piers that support them. Nevertheless, the feeling created by this building when viewed along Eastgate is one of exhilaration. It seems likely however that the effect will be weakened: instead of preserving this vista, plans are afoot to build an hotel and a multi-storey car park on the open area to the west front of Quarry House.

Park Square

In the later 18th century, commercial and professional families began the construction of terraces and squares of houses close to the town centre. Park Place, East Parade and South Parade were all once fashionable districts of Leeds. Park Square was begun around 1788. This, together with many more Leeds houses and a further selection of industrial, commercial and public buildings, will be contained in the second part of *Leeds: the Architectural Heritage* which Ryburn will publish later in 1993.